Strange Hymn

Strange Hymn

CARLENE KUCHARCZYK

UNIVERSITY OF MASSACHUSETTS PRESS

AMHERST AND BOSTON

ISBN 978-1-62534-864-7 (paper)

Designed by Jen Jackowitz
Set in Centaur
Printed and bound by Books International, Inc.

Cover design by adam b. bohannon
Cover photo by unknown, vintage choir robe, circa 1930. Public Domain.

Library of Congress Cataloging-in-Publication Data

Names: Kucharczyk, Carlene, 1988- author
Title: Strange hymn / Carlene Kucharczyk.
Description: Amherst : University of Massachusetts Press, [2025] | Series:
Juniper prize for poetry |
Identifiers: LCCN 2024035434 (print) | LCCN 2024035435 (ebook) | ISBN
9781625348647 paperback | ISBN 9781685751425 ebook | ISBN 9781685751432
epub
Subjects: LCGFT: Poetry
Classification: LCC PS3611.U295 S77 2025 (print) | LCC PS3611.U295
(ebook) | DDC 811/.6—dc23/eng/20241127
LC record available at https://lccn.loc.gov/2024035434
LC ebook record available at https://lccn.loc.gov/2024035435

British Library Cataloguing-in-Publication Data
A catalog record for this book is available from the British Library.

for you

CONTENTS

Strange Hymn

church

body,   go reverently

                              submerged

in love

        little human cathedral

                              (*all* this)

to be wholly occupied

                      with the singing—

On Beholding the Beloved's Rotting Body

I think it is beautiful that Emerson
dug his wife out of the grave
a year and two months after she died
just to see how she was making out.
Perhaps I would have liked to marry
Emerson. This is not the first time
I have thought this. I think I would do well
with a staunch moralist type. Unless
of course I disagreed, which I likely
often would. I do not really like
beards anyway. But now I am looking
at a picture of Emerson and it seems
he had less of a beard and more
of just weird facial hair. I do not know
what this particular type is called,
I do not like it either. Perhaps I was
thinking of Thoreau. I am always thinking
of Thoreau. But back to Emerson's wife.
Maybe he thought she was caught
somewhere between the skeleton
and the soul. She was only twenty
years old. Who knows. I would not
mind. Find it all out. Dig if you have to.

The Sirens

—after the Edward Burne-Jones painting

i

The moment before it happens
should be a good one. Mouths flopping,

water, water, or a prayer. And yet,
look at us—dreary, bored—whitely lighted,

ready to braid anchors with our hair.
We could learn to breathe the sea, wind it
into our lungs. And Odysseus?

Not tied to the mast with waxen ears, not
in the cabin. Climb the cliffs,

not the tendriled seaweed. The anchors *like*
to drown deeply. Let them. Dying and rising,

dying and rising, like gods. Lanterns release
to the first-born wind. Look

closely: your next look will be of corpses.

ii

Concern brushed onto you. Will you
accept it? Uncover your mouth.

NO ONE IS SINGING

Island of ghosts, *hushed,* nicely tucked
among the feathered beds of eternity.

      Ocean.   That's all.

Farewell solo gull, sleep well among the winds,
tread water, peck bits of skin
from whales' backs. *Something.* Heartache

is boundless; time is boundlessness. Working
clocks on the ocean floor. Only two
have seen. Only three have heard.

(Something I shouldn't have told you.)

Well then: the wrong dead hour. No way
to measure minutes. Need rope! *See* me. Look

closely: your next look will be before time.

iii

—Oh, we were just waiting in a gilded room,

wanted to make something of our hands,

found them in each other. Trying to think:

subordinate driftwood. Moonless night,

heard a harp—don't know where. Meet us.

The room above the ocean. Swing. Make sure

you jump. Dance. Make sure you fall. Drown.

Make sure you sink. Into the ballroom.

Moonbeam, a window, lovely sure death.

Don't look down. Waiting. *For what?* Look

closely: your next look will be of abstinence.

song

the other things of earth, okay   I like
the thing that is your body   buried now
in deathless sleep   sunken in midnight quiet

I am awake in wonder of   what rows
its dreamboats through your mind   what floating world
drifts away   but what world is this in which

you ever die   hours haunted by the ringing
of church bells   flocks of birds in wild whorls
the sounds of spring unwrapping   streets lamp-lit

if I could be with you   the whole way singing

Dark Corner

At the once-beautiful hotel we try to eat breakfast;
there is only an egg still in its shell,
you can have it.
I tell the man the coffee's gone.
He assures me two minutes
and disappears into the backroom.

You used to work at a hotel,
sixteen, in and out of guests' rooms, collecting trays,
hello, thank you, have a nice day.
Once, you brought eggs to a man
and when he turned around after signing the bill,
the tie on his bathrobe slipped.

I watch the bar across the room:
only the ghosts of ghosts are drinking this morning,
not a rowdy bunch,
tired from their night-travels in and out of strangers' rooms,
never touching the furniture,
only the sleeping faces that have forgotten the bodies they belong to.

Damaged sofas line the halls of the seven floors.
No one touches them
except for wandering or waiting children,
who, when left to themselves, are not afraid of things
damaged and worn.

Years from now, at the hotel liquidators,
people will see these couches and say yes, yes,
this is exactly the type of thing you would find in an old hotel.
They will buy more domestic pieces,
a chair with yellow upholstery from the St. Regis,
a small carafe to put flowers or milk in,
a painting for a bedroom.

I tell you, I wish we could stay here longer
in this hotel of lost grandeur, this palace of interesting disarray,
and stay here with these pieces of the impersonal past
that have somehow not yet outlasted their small lights.

Twenty minutes later,
the man brings out the coffee.
He smiles and says he almost forgot,
as if once again surprising himself.

October Snow

When we arrived at the funeral home, it began
to snow, suggesting to us the sun too had trouble

heaving its great body from bed that morning. It too
was suffering *in the startled space which a youth*

as lovely as a god has suddenly left forever—you
didn't look like you, your head so badly bruised

it could not be concealed. At night, verses flew
at me with more wind than ever. I let them come,

transcribed them from their first airy dictation,
threw off the body's desire for sleep. I let them

bury themselves in my bed, my hair, my head,
wherever they could find rest in this temporary home

of my body. I sought to separate a part of myself,
whether it was the mind, the soul, the spirit. I wanted

to know at once and definitively our animal bodies
were not all we were. It is shameful to be this fragile.

Moonvine

It opens as distant twilight gallops in;
nightfall, the bursting white grows ghost,
the unexpected host of the startled vine,
floating above or twining down below

the trellis and window. The urgent trembling
into bloom: each night, another birth.
A paper bird of many wings unfolding,
the hollow center catches and thirsts

for life beyond itself: moonglow, visitors
who drift or stumble in and sleep all day,
perhaps unexpectedly having to wait
for night in the nook of the shadowed face.

Evening, you can ask it with your hands
to spread early—it might. A slight touch
can start a life. Dawn, it shudders back
into itself. A Morning Glory unfurls.

Lady Agnes

—after the Herman Hesse fairytale "Shadow Play"

A woman werewolf, the Baron's brother said.
A saint, the old women said. *Pick me up,*
the children begged. *We live in this castle*
like shadows, the poet Floribert said, kept saying.
Heads bowed out from windows toward
the incantatory cabin where she slept, the wind
helped itself to bread, the children helped
themselves to her hands. The story moved forward
with birches, boats, handsome men, but always
a shadow somewhere lurking, seeping in
through the damp walls, circling the blue
mountains. Inside the dead house, the poet stirred:
We live in this castle like shadows, not men,
filled his head. He didn't write it down;
he brought the first tea roses to her bed. Night
after night, men in boats brought her where
they wanted. Everything was okay until it wasn't.

Mary

MARY HELD HER HANDS WIDE OPEN

I reached out to them.

To the hands of Mary on the hill at my great-grandma's house.
Mary at the top of the hill, Mary at the edge of the woods, Holy
Mary, Mary Mother of God, Mary, Mary, Mary. *In every church
Mary held her white hands open*, I find written in a poem. My version
would be: *On the hill Mary held her hands wide open.* I would sometimes
walk up to her and kneel. I remember quite liking her.

MARY DOESN'T LIKE IT WHEN I PEE AND SING

And I don't like Mary. Mary's a tyrant. Making me feel ashamed
for singing while I pee. Even if it is her house. Okay, I did like
Mary, elementary school Mary. But I didn't like that she made me
feel embarrassed for singing while I peed.

I lie, I tell her I wasn't. I say I was only singing *before* I peed and that
I stopped to go to the bathroom. She says no, I heard you singing
and peeing at the same time. She insists: *I heard the singing and the pee.*

MARY COMES OVER TO MY HOUSE

I don't know that she ever did.

She must have, right?

MY FIRST MARY

My first Mary was my great-aunt Mary, my mom's aunt. She lived in Ohio. We sent her videos and letters. And possibly Flat Stanley. We drove from Connecticut to visit her. She lived with her brother. After she died, he moved to Alaska and began building a cabin.

We went to her house and took some things to remember her by. I took a black crescent moon ring and little shirts (I don't know what else to call them), red, navy, and white, that were supposed to make it look like you were wearing a turtleneck when you weren't.

NOTE TO MARY

Mary?

Mary?

Mary, why don't you answer back?

BLOODY MARY

Let's not start with Mary, let's start with Chelsea. The kids in elementary school made fun of Chelsea. She was new to the school and had blonde, almost white, hair, and blue eyes. Someone said she was albino. It caught on. Everyone said she had a "pig nose."

Chelsea told us about Bloody Mary. You were supposed to spin around three times in front of the mirror and say something, and again, and then she would appear. I never tried. I was too scared. I don't know if Chelsea did either.

MISTAKEN FOR MARY

I don't remember ever having been. Do you?

MARY, MARY ON THE WALL

Mary, Mary on the wall. Why would Mary be on the wall? How long has she been there?

No, not Mary on the wall, *Mirror* on the wall. *Mirror, Mirror on the wall.*

An honest mistake. We need not ask the question why Mary is on the wall.

QUESTION FOR MARY

Mary, won't you let us raise our glasses to you?

No, Mary isn't interested in the raising of glasses. She'd rather you kept your glasses down.

THE INTERSECTION OF MARYS

This one is yours to write. Fill it in here.

THINGS I HAVEN'T HEARD ABOUT MARY

- Mary had a brilliant bosom.
- Mary left you and she doesn't want to come back (the possibilities of Mary).
- Mary was mildly resentful, but did not at all act on those feelings.
- Mary doesn't love you and never did. (For someone this resonates; I'm sorry.)

MARY TYLER MOORE

My friend is surprised I don't know who Mary Tyler Moore is. He says she is a big deal, that she was the first woman to wear pants on a television show, that she refused to be on it if she couldn't wear pants, I should know who she is.

FORGOTTEN MARYS

There are many, I admit, that I have forgotten, or purposefully left out, for different reasons.

A space for them.

Specifically, this one here: .

THINGS I WON'T TELL YOU ABOUT MARY

Nothing. I'll tell you everything I know. Though there might not be much to tell. Remember, I am not myself a Mary, only an observer of Marys, a collector of Marys, and a recent one at that.

THE SORROWING VIRGIN

I didn't know at first that it was Mary, as she was going by another name. What a thing to be known as—The Sorrowing Virgin. And so . . . publicly. Why must the virgin sorrow? Why mustn't the virgin triumph? I know, I know the story. And I admit there is a certain ring to The Sorrowing Virgin, but surely there are better things she could be called. Isn't there also a certain ring to The Triumphing Virgin? The Ecstatic Virgin? The Virgin of Ecstasy?

The Sorrowing Virgin's eyes are made of glass beads and are raised skyward, making her look possessed, which leads me to the question: Can sorrow possess you? Can it make a possession of you? Can it inhabit you so you are no longer your own? If we are ever our own?

Can sorrow make a home of you the way we are making a home of Mary? What is the process like and how long does it take? Can sorrow burrow into a person over time? Or does it sometimes cut a hole right through?

I found Mary because I was looking for my friend in the museum. I thought she *was* my friend for a moment. I consider if my friend would be more of a Magdalene or a Virgin. I decide she would not really be either Mary. I'm sure there is a more fitting one.

QUICK DETOUR—RODIN'S HANDS

At the museum I also see Rodin's hands. I wonder if he ever sculpted Mary—that is, her hands—and if her fingers were long or short—that is, whichever particular Mary he sculpted. He may have sculpted the hands of many Marys.

Rodin thought the creative life involved suffering and martyrdom, and I might agree. I'm still deciding.

I find out he sculpted Christ and Mary Magdalene, which I did not know, and this one I did not see. I'm sorry, I only wanted to find a way to include Rodin's hands—that is, the ones he sculpted, not his own. I wonder if he sculpted his own.

MARY AND HER SEVEN BEDRAGGLED DEVILS

Marie Howe in her poem "Magdalene—The Seven Devils" tells us about Mary Magdalene's seven devils. Some are rotating; they are given up and then replaced, sometimes with ones that are only slightly different. It seems true we get rid of one devil only to replace it with the next.

Some of my favorite devils in the poem are:

- *that no one knew me, although they thought they did. And that if people thought of me as little as I thought of them then what was love?*
- *that the dead seemed more alive to me than the living*
- *I didn't think you, if I told you, would understand any of this.*

- She is often busy and considers this a devil. This is repeated throughout the poem.
- *that I projected onto others what I myself was feeling.*
- *I knew I was breathing the expelled breath of everything that was alive and I couldn't stand it.*
- *The seventh was the way my mother looked when she was dying—her mouth wrenched into an O so as to take in as much air . . .*

Mary, I hear if you look at your devils (yes, just glance back at them), they won't have as much power over you.

Mary and I, we have some of the same devils. But mostly we have different ones.

There is not always a devil floating near. Often the air seems clear of devils and I can breathe easy, even while knowing I am breathing the expelled breath of everything that was alive. (Honestly, this isn't something I often think about, and when I do I find it comforting.)

THE PROBLEM WITH MARY

There are many. I think we just discussed some. Would you like to add anything?

MARY IS DOING VERY WELL FOR HERSELF

Someone's said this, I'm sure.

MARY IS VERY MUCH SO

Whatever it is you're thinking, Mary is. Very much so. I say in a convincing tone.

WHAT'S IN MARY

An army. An arm. A yam. A ram. A ray. Ma. Amy. May. Am.

WHAT MARY'S IN

Marty. Martyr. Martyrdom. Martyred. Marry. Marilyn. Army.

Martyr only has one additional letter than Mary (and the repeated "r"). This leads me to the question: Are Marys often mistaken for martyrs? It seems they might be.

I do not know if she wants to be in the army, but it's such a perfect fit.

Mary and I have two of the same letters in our first names, but Mary cannot fit into me, nor I into her.

MARY IN LETTERS

I am reading the letters of the Clairmont family. Most of them are written to Mary Shelley's stepsister, Claire Clairmont, and are from her nephew, Wilhelm. Mary Shelley never appears in the letters, not by name. So far in my reading of them, the Shelleys are referred to only once.

I feel a strong connection to Mary Shelley and her mother, also a Mary, Mary Wollstonecraft—I feel a stronger connection to Wollstonecraft than Shelley. I love her letters the most, which seem to show her exquisite Maryness more than her other writing.

The Clairmonts often sign their letters "Believe me, dearest . . ." and then some affectionate saying, like "Yours affectly." They are mostly unlike the Marys, not because of how they sign their letters, but because of what they think.

MARY OF THE MOOR

I don't know of any, but I'm sure there was one. What about *The Secret Garden*? Was there a Mary in that? There certainly was a moor.

I can see it now—Mary is tidying up the moor again. Mary is making a mess of the moor again. The moor is all Mary's. Mary is making more of a mess. She is making the moor a mess. She is making more of a mess of the moor!

In the Clairmont letters, a lovely typo: "Once Moor Goodbye." I think they do this more than once. I don't remember for certain who is responsible for the lovely typo. I think perhaps it was Wilhelm.

MARY OF THE WINDOWS

No, it wasn't Mary; it was Mother of the Windows and Emily Dickinson wrote it in a letter. Her mother wasn't a Mary, nor was her sister Lavinia. And she certainly wasn't; she was an Emily Dickinson!

MOTHER OF THE MARYS

I don't think she exists. If she does, I certainly am not her. Although in this essay, perhaps I am the mother. Yes, I am mother to the Marys in this essay. What would these Marys be called?

- Marys of the Essay (which?)
- Marys Who Only Exist in Essay Form (too academic)
- Marys Who Live in the Essay (reminds me of *The Indian in the Cupboard*)
- Marys Who Live in Essays (inclusive, other essays, and so, inaccurate)
- Marys of This Essay (perhaps the most accurate, but I don't like the way it sounds and aesthetics are important)

MARY AS REBEL

Of all the meanings of the name Mary (*bitterness, beloved, wished-for child*), *rebelliousness* is the one I like best. Mary is a rebel. In Mary a rebellion stirs. A rebel is Mary.

MARY AS SAINT

At the silent meditation retreat, we are told, if we like, we can pick a saint or figure to inspire us. It does not occur to me to choose Mary. I learn later we were actually told *not* to do this, so it is good that I did not.

MARY AS REBEL-SAINT

Aren't saints a sort of rebel, really? They are certainly rebelling from the norm. This is an imagined Mary—but she's the one I think I would like best.

A more appealing version of sainthood, not the type most oft depicted, by G. K. Chesterton: *Virtue is not the absence of vices or the avoidance of moral dangers; virtue is a vivid and separate thing, like pain or a particular smell. . . . Chastity does not mean abstention from sexual wrong; it means something flaming, like Joan of Arc.*

I imagine Mary has some of this peculiar wild flame. Mary is good-fiery. Fiery-good.

And everywhere.

The Language of Fairytales

What will we do with the hour before the wolf comes?

(worlds on top of this one)   Everything is green

very green here   Stalks stir in the night   Should

we sleep entwined in the vines   see if we wake?

throttled by the stalk   I grow wild in the night

like woods like roots like hair   Exit this place

with me   (yes, the world)   It is strange

very strange here   I wait for the one who sleeps

a hundred years   Everything everything has an echo

Elk float freely by the bank   Silver slipper spilled

onto you   Seething sister bites into you   Merry

merry singing men   Long live the dead queen

Rapunzel,   pull back your hair   I will take

your firstborn (   )   I do not like it here I do

not like it here   Though that woman looking at me

through the trees   *is*   strange and lovely . . .

Ode to Eventide

Alles Nahe werde fern. —Goethe

Everything near becomes distant. Sweet V of geese.
You, running off the horizon, hair blown back

by wind. Everything you love has left this house.
Is burning. *Everything near becomes distant.* A dark snow

has fallen, has changed the world so completely
you could not claim it as your own. *Everything*

near becomes distant. Your face, the moon now.
Still glowing. Unreachable. Even for my hands.

Aubade in Orange

I would wake to you another morning if I could,
watch our souls slip out of our bodies, float
over this city, rise with the dawn.
I would buy you a whole fruit basket if I could,
but there's nowhere to get one, nothing is open.
Except your mouth, your mouth is open.

I could sing to you if you wanted, I don't have to.
You can tell me, anything you like, I'll listen.
I want to keep warm with you,
I want us to put sadness to sleep, once and for all,
I hear it needs a good long rest.
This city is always sleeping, I am sad for it,
it does not know what it feels like to be awake.
I want to sing the blueness out of you.
                    Could you sing the blueness out of me too?
The city, I want to sing the blueness out of it too.
Let's sing sadness back to sleep.
I want to make a clean break from it, once and for all.
A fruit basket, to show my love is a brightly colored thing.
It sings and sings, it will go on singing, this morning it will sing.
For you, for you, my one sweet love, for you.
It sings and sings, it will go on singing, this morning it will sing.
Who to call for a fruit basket for you, for you, for you, for you,
my one sweet love, for you?

Do Not Hold the Birds

Do not hold the birds, do not make
little homes of your hands, do not ache
into a man. He will be silent
until spring, when love again
blasts through the sodden heart.

It is not good to bury all the bones
in the yard, it is not good to keep
all one's favorite books on the shelf. Give
both hands to the birds. Lend them.

Ode to Shoulders

They stand, two tall tents
side by side. A fire in between
and a little north. The fire
is your mouth. It burns,
I kiss you, pour water,
it smolders. It is easy
to love a man from the back,
shoulders representative
of the body. My own, thin,
even when I am not.
Not so obviously sexual
as the breasts, the sex.
Leading the body or held
back in repose. Shoulders,
lend me your grace, let you
stand for the whole.

All the Girls Were There, and Gorgeous

All the girls were there, and gorgeous,
my grandmother says, from her bed
at the Alzheimer's center.
I admire the poetry of her words,
the unusual syntax, the regular meter:
all the girls were there, and gorgeous.

I wonder which year she is in, which room.
I imagine the girls are dancing.
I imagine my grandfather there.
I wonder if he notices any of the girls
are gorgeous except for her.

My grandmother, whose hair
was once so thick the rain bounced off it, she said.
My grandfather, who loved her
more than she loved him.

I remember their bickering, how it made
us sad. I could not have made it
with anyone else, she said.

I kiss her cheek, I hold
her cracked hands. They are always dry.
I wonder about the part of her that is here,
the part that is elsewhere.
We do not like to visit her,
I hope she does not know.

All the gorgeous girls are leaving,
but my grandmother remains,
awake in her life, though
she doesn't know it.

the crow

brother

brother

it was not love

that made you

shoot that crow

(I do not like

them either)

when it fell

from the sky

your friend Mike

said its blood

looked like Cheetos

tell me

did you then

not want to cry?

you didn't

remember

you told me

about the coyote

how you couldn't find him

how you traveled

his trail of blood

how you said

that night

you couldn't sleep

brother

brother

tonight

we were laughing

and you didn't

seem to mind

you didn't

even get that mad

when I asked

why

you killed

that crow

you said

remember

you said

you weren't saying

it was the right thing

to do

All Souls

It is 1988 and I have no idea what you're wearing. I wasn't born yet. What did you wear then? In pictures, you are smiling, have short hair. I was born at night—eleven something. I've never known how close it was to not being All Souls' Day, end of fall, the skeleton trees already speaking of winter with their undressed branches.

I am five. I love my mom. I write it at school. By this age, you had already lost your mom. Twenty years later I ask you about my earliest memories and you tell me yours: you remember taking a bath with your mom, then later going to the hospital. Was she already gone when you got there?

You lose a tooth. No one cares. You wiggle another one out. No one cares. The last one comes out. No one notices. You and your sister search the house for something to eat, taking tiny scoops of peanut butter, whatever could easily go unnoticed. Your stepmom does notice and you will paint the garage for it that summer.

There will be no music to listen to while you paint. You will not love The Beatles. You will not sing, "Why don't we do it in the road?" You will sing your own song, but it will come later. Later, later, it will come later. Later, you will learn to sing.

i do not remember much
about that winter

she does not know everything about me

that girl upstairs

whom i have never seen

but only hear

for example

i am very quiet when i come

i do not think

anyone could hear me

i have always been

there are people who do quiet everything

i am not them

i have not the quietest quietest mouth

the orthodontist said

you have got

an abnormal amount of saliva

in your mouth

your small mouth

with big teeth

i met someone else

with too much saliva

i said, we can never make out

that was that

a red jacket for Christmas

a bag under the tree

from the office

it was mine

i had lost it

then i had it back

that was that

me and jacket again

he was dead though

i went to someone else

i do not remember much

about that winter

or i do

but only in fragments

i think of separately

and cannot say

they belong to that winter

because i cannot tell you even

which winter that was

did i say he was dead

not the other person

with too much saliva

the orthodontist

dr griener

yes an odd name

for an orthodontist

being very close

to grinder

which is not

what you want

to happen

to your teeth

grind grind grind

grind grind

grind

i remember that office

actually very well

the waiting room

there were fish

i think

i was always thinking

about something

very stupid

in that room

waiting

to get the elastics

on my braces changed

waiting

to not need them

Curtains

The light they let in, the light they keep out.
    The darkness that fills the room after the drama
of their great closures. The shuffle as they drift

across the floor, holding themselves together.
    Rembrandt, Monet, playing with light. Blocking
time, then bringing it back. The sheer ones

that can't quite keep the morning out. Some, thick
    enough to sleep in. The higher they are, the taller
the room appears. Gatekeepers, gathering the light,

then giving it back. Their rods span arches. Hemming
    ours, I cried on the floor. It wasn't how I wanted
to spend Saturday. The sun shoveling in, the gold

curtains glistening on the floor, waiting to be hung,
    waiting for the scene to finish. What was it then
that would not shine for me? I live in a house

without curtains now, my windows let in what others
    keep out: the intruding stars, the brooding duskiness,
the shadows that often appear without an overture.

The Agony in the Garden

Lord, you look more haunted
than I have seen you before

as if El Greco had cast himself
into the white of your eyes, his

singular dark glow transforming
your figure, spreading his light

over the eerie trees and deepening
the rock that echoes your shape,

the oblong figures and moonlit clouds,
the iceberg madness reigning above

the angel draped in a yellow robe,
wings like those of Leda's swan,

holding the cup of Passion, knowing
it will not alter the course of things,

the task will still remain: the men
already moving the plot deathward.

In Medias Res

We all—in the end—die in medias res.
In the middle of a story. Of many stories.

—Mona Simpson

In the middle of a good night's sleep the middle
of an intersection the middle of dinner the middle
of a kitchen floor the middle of a hotel room you didn't
intend to stay in the middle of an evening the middle
of a conversation the middle of rush hour the others
coming and going you with them there then gone
the middle of a foreign country the middle of a war
you knew nothing of the middle of a heist the middle
of your son's first year of high school the middle
of a fight the middle of a recession the middle of a book
the middle of a century the middle of the Appalachian
Trail the middle of the end the middle of your husband's
life the middle of a birth the middle of the late-night
hospital shift the middle of a dark street the middle
of a good love the middle of a cup of coffee the middle
of sabbatical the middle of a sleepless night the middle
of an ice storm in the middle of winter the middle
of a swimming pool the middle of your wife's retirement
the middle of the afternoon the middle of a guest room
the middle of the semester and then into the middle
of the earth dirt resting below and above you into
the middle of a place suspicious and new into the middle
of white or ghosts or angels or nothingness into the middle

of knowledge or wisdom or omniscience or peace or into
the middle of nowhere into the middle of eternity into
the middle of the great past or thrust into the middle
of someone else's story or into the middle of some animal's
good strong body the middle always the middle edging
toward the end and away from the beginning but lost
somewhere in the middle at the intersection of many middles.

[you were in the world]

you were
in the world

the same time
I was

we could
have been

less lonely
together

*

in the heart
of the beloved

is a city
that never sleeps

it is named
after you

*

in all your lives
you were frightened

in all your loves
you were whole

*

I did not think

it would take so long

for me to find you

I did not think
it would take so long

for you to pass

*

in the eyes
of the beloved

I am
the most I'll ever be

*

with love
there is no substitute
for time

*

when you visit
my body

I
am delighted

*

perhaps my heartsong
is not specific

perhaps it looks
for anyone
to sing to

*

it is love
or it is not

we will see

*

you lie asleep
in my heart

waiting
to be woken

*

when I awoke
it was always to you

even when
you were not there

*

I was a wish
swimming in a river

you washed
over me

*

love, I know
none of this now

nor did I then

*

I have loved you
in the looseness of the dark

but perhaps
never so much
as in the mornings

when we were
beginning something
together

Self-Portrait through Glass

How many people came and stayed a certain time,
Uttered light or dark speech that became part of you
Like light behind windblown fog and sand,
Filtered and influenced by it, until no part
Remains that is surely you

*

her leaving a doorway, light leaving a doorway

SHE

Is that her? Is that me?

See, see her there . . .

                You didn't miss her, did you?

The self winks at me in the mirror. She calls to me from behind the glass. I think she's inviting us in.

Let's enter:

She

she she she   she she   she is me

so,   she

        cannot be defined by thee!

                      (me!)

Someone else must judge

this one's identity

      (ha ha—this time not me)

I hope they *judge tenderly*

          of me.

I feel myself coming out of myself.
    The glass begins to shatter.

I feel myself coming out of myself.
    The glass begins to shatter.

I feel myself coming out of myself.
    The glass begins to shatter.

People who live in glass houses should not write poems.

But what if they don't want to live in glass houses? What if they're desperately trying to break out of them? Can they write poems then?

Yes, technically they still live in glass houses, but the glass, the glass begins to shatter . . .

(If you acquiesce to my writing a poem, then this: huge swarming essay-poem of selfdom, kingdom of self, yes, where I live, strange existence, tiring sometimes too.)

Is a mirror a sort of glass house?

And, is there a way to see ourselves besides through the glass?

UNMOORED

I was feeling unmoored, boat at sea, tilted, yes, that was me. Dipping, dripping, waves, wee, sun in eyes, mermaid gleam, sailor sheen, falling, sailing, boating, shoring, sterling seas, big breeze, seaward please!

All aboard.

All aboard.

All aboard.

I feel myself coming out of myself.
The glass begins to shatter.

I feel myself coming out of myself.
The glass begins to shatter.

I feel myself coming out of myself.
The glass begins to shatter.

Borges: no self!

Fitzgerald: no self!   (and, I want to die)

Kunitz: *some principle of being abides*

(all three sailed on the ship with me, we sang together in the sea, Fitzgerald not merry, tried to join the sirens, but we wouldn't let he!)

BE

Maybe when one unattaches from the self, one is free to be *be birds flying, be the enormous movements of the snows, be rain, be love*

Maybe there is also an opportunity to be woodsmoke passed from fire, now dangling in hair that sweeps over shower water, be wind rising, be the cracking sheets of ice, be all the good around you, go unnoticed, submit to everything, be the brilliant gales of flight, be the all-night torches of young love, be staid love's constancy and promise, be the shadows that scare you don't turn from them in the dark, be God, be breath, be the intensity of longing, be trees yes be the trees pines oaks willows swaying, be dark water hitting the shore, be the turtles that come out at night guide themselves to the ocean then never see each other again, be each wind that swooped to kiss you, be images classical and grand, be bridges, be cathedrals, be the sound of trains, *be rain, be love*

Anything, one can be, after getting rid of the burden of the self (not straight death, he he, an ego death persee!)—a ridding of that uncertain certainty
Then, no one as expansive as thee!

And then with Borges one can sing in ecstasy of the nothingness of personality.

Show me,
how expansive can thee be?

I feel myself coming out of myself.
    The glass begins to shatter.

I feel myself coming out of myself.
    The glass begins to shatter.

I feel myself coming out of myself.
    The glass begins to shatter.

I & THOU

In bed I try to feel Thou come into me,

Is this Thou then me?

(Thou infinite white primordial being)

Why do I invite this Thou to me?

Is He even larger than me?

Maybe me (she!) is just as large as He!

Dare we . . . larger than He?

Thou is certainly not as free as me! weeeee

Sh. *My business is to sing*

What do I sing of?

Of course, me!

Will I sing now?

Yes, indeed!

How?

Ecstatically!

SELF-PORTRAIT SINGING

My calves are singing. Eyes. Shoulders. Elbows. Blood rivering
through singing:

I want to be uncompromising. I want to be the most uncompro-
mising woman in the world.

What I want is uncompromised singing.

In me also is the animal that glistens and rushes toward us.

Wolf in my ear. Wolf at my side. Wolf on my back. Winter's
sweeping howls. Snow here already. Singing.

Night, song of many owls lifting, wind burns into me. My hands,
numb, are singing.

When sleeping, the shadow part, the part *dark and smart*, goes on
singing its own strange song.

The lyrics are: I am part of you too, lower yourself into the well,
then pull yourself back up.

All my life I've been singing.

Of course, you cannot always hear my song.

Sometimes the lights, and music too, go out.

I am a dark house.

But there beating, beating below in the basement is a bright-
winged bird that lives and wants to get out.

Flapping, flapping, in my chest now.

Out of my throat flies the bird, fully loaded with song.

I turn to watch the black speck in the distance, still singing.

One day I'll die alone singing.

You too, keep working on your song.

When I'm afraid, singing.

The lyrics are, *Let everything happen to you: beauty and terror.*

Song of naming things:

Beauty.

Terror.

Beauty.

Terror.

Beauty.

Terror.

Would it all fit in?

I want you to sing yourself into me. Sing your best song, the one you'd like to hear, I'll listen.

The lyrics are: It is rare that we should be here, it is rare that we should have met.

The lyrics are: I want us to be invested in what is good for one another.

The lyrics are: I am grateful to have heard your song.

I want to stay with you all night singing.

I can hear your bones singing. Breath. Your eyes, they know so many songs. I want to learn them all.

My voice has many moods.

Sometimes it is not so much my voice as someone's who is hovering slightly above me, someone I am reaching for.

Don't mistake my singing. You have your own song.

My favorite thing about you was that night you were singing what
sounded like a hymn.

Where did it come from?

It was then I knew you could be much more than you were.

After I'm gone, don't bury my body—

Burn it, and turn it into song.

LOVE

Can we best be defined by what we love? What loves us perhaps?

I could not tell you what loves me, but I can tell you what I love . . .

I love the leaping eyes of children, how they let their incorrigible gazes stay on you.

I love people who are humanizing. They are the best kind.

I love what is happening in the woods right now.

Consider the possibilities (let the many sets of eyes tell you: ravenous, alert, frightened, calm).

I love the lilting wind, the bend and sway of trees above graves. I love those graves, the people that might have lived.

I love thinking of the dead. But also I love the living. There is nothing like the living. (The dead, though, they had their chance.)

I love the strangeness of churches, all those people chanting together things they don't understand, don't believe in. Borges saying the trinity is an intellectual horror. A specious infinity. Two mirrors lain side by side.

I love cathedrals. Reverence in any form.

The rain—I think I would have loved it as soon as I knew it. But when did I first know it?

Don't assume I love you.

Even though I love much and nonexclusively, I may not be able to find a place for you in my heart.

Okay, I admit: I am happy you are here.

. . . but what is the quality of my love for you?

Is it birds at night beating their wings against a black sky, the still-
ness of trees in a dead wind, the silence of memories forgotten,
a hollowing out of the ribs, breath easy, breathing more?

Is it the Vs of geese, always always receding, balloon moving higher
into the sky, arrow accidentally shot and leaping behind the
pines, deeper into the forest? Is my love for you always moving?

Is it loud and boisterous like a children's party, and is there a swing
that keeps moving back and forth and will not stop, though it is
sometimes lesser, sometimes more?

Whatever it is exactly, it is a love of spaces. I love love that has
spaces. There are many holes in my love.

I do not want to be the only thing you love, but I would like to
have some part in all the things you love.

If it is possible for me to love them too, then my part also will be
in loving them.

Earth is the right place for love, Robert Frost wrote, *I don't know where it's
likely to go better.*

It has been said he was not very good at love. Maybe its absence is
what haunted him.

I am not at all at ease in the world, but there are moments it is easy,
I am free.

These moments I feel a love that is more grateful than loving.
Relief resides there too, feeling of homecoming.

I cannot see an end to my love, but I cannot always find its
presence. Sometimes its place is taken by

HATE

It seems cruel to define me by what I hate, but if this is how you choose to define me, I must tell you what I hate.

(I do not feel any hatred now, so this may not seem honest, but perhaps a gleam of the old hatred will find its way in.)

I do not hate death in general, but there are certain kinds of death I hate.

I hate easily avoidable deaths. I hate death that seems ironic. Trivial deaths. Absurd deaths.

The young boy eaten by the woodchipper in a moment. The father there, nothing for him to grab after. Just. Gone.

The girl walking on the street, something falling on her from above.

These types of death seem to mock life, beautiful and exuberant. And it is difficult for me to see their beauty. I don't.

But even worse than random deaths are cruel deaths. The mother tickling the baby at the concentration camp, so he will laugh before they're shot. How is it that they should be there? What series of events led to this?

(I always think of this scene at the concentration camp because I cannot think of anything worse.)

Could you imagine being there and somehow loving it? What would it be like to love it?

Would you tell yourself about the strangeness of humans, of life . . . how mysterious, how *interesting*?

Could that translate into beauty? Could you make curiosity a form of prayer?

Or would you have to look at everything as though it were very distant, as if you were somewhere very far away, somewhere in space? What kind of lens would you need for this? The eye of a scientist? stoic? writer?

Perhaps Keats could find the beauty, *I have loved the principle of beauty in all things*, he said.

But that does not mean that there *is* the principle of beauty in all things. Perhaps he is just saying when he has found the principle of beauty, he has loved it.

Or perhaps the terrible thing itself does not contain beauty, but there is beauty there in spite of (the mother tickling the baby).

I hate war. It is hard for me to believe it happens (I am lucky for this distance).

I try to imagine its first spark—to look at it on the level of individuals, as a Jane Austen novel would.

I see two faces aglow in night. I see someone not knowing what to do with silence, the sometimes starkness of it. (I hope it was not me in another life, or later in this one.)

I think of men who damage and destroy to feel.

If you feel this way, as you sometimes might, think of the most innocent child you can imagine and it will make you want to do only good. Somewhere this person exists (maybe it was you once).

Sometimes I hate the things I say—when they are trite or dull or false. Sometimes, before they leave my mouth, I already know I do not want to say them.

Though this list is not inclusive, I will end here because one should not think too much on hate, especially when one does not feel it.

Perhaps galloping next to hate (riding on two scraggly horses side by side) is

FEAR

It also seems cruel to define me by what I fear.

However, if this is how you choose to define me, I must tell you what I fear.

The fear that I feel most is the fear that I, or anyone I love, can at any moment, be pulled out of the house of life forever.

Fear seems a natural response to this condition. Who could say this was not terrifying? And who could tell you it was otherwise?

Yet to live fully with this fear I think is possible.

I am sometimes afraid of my shadow (or shadows, twice I have seen *three* walking with me).

I am afraid of becoming a caricature.

Often in a place with many people, I look at them and see each carrying their own unique affectations.

It is easy to tell when someone is wearing these affectations.

I have felt them too on my own face. And I am terrified they will become my permanent face, that someday I will not be able to take them off.

It will have happened gradually, but there will be a moment when I notice it, or maybe I (more terrifyingly) will not notice. I will have lost my ability to realize it is not my face.

What a relief it is to meet an open and plain face. I can think of some I've seen now, those brief sanctuaries of existence.

Look at the animals, in particular their eyes, passing from one
fearful moment to the next, thrown by some strange wind in
and out of existence.

Dark stream of fear. It can flood. It can swallow everything. (Don't
let it.)

Sometimes it grows strong, but it will not always have such
strength.

Are you, do you think, more afraid than me?

Where do you keep your fear? Is it often buried beneath your
breastbone? Do you try to dig it out?

Some nights I have not been able to sleep, imagining my parents'
impending deaths.

I do not know why at those times the fact that they would die, that
I would be left here alone without them, those two who knew
me so well, struck me so.

It seemed a deep horror, and in my bed, fear spread its wings
around me.

It kept gathering, gathering, a great party (so many invitations sent,
everyone came). I felt quite fragile wrapped in it.

I have talked to others and they have before been enclosed in this
same fear—haunted space of twigs and bones, no homecoming.

I am afraid of being misunderstood, of being thought awful,
because not understood, and of being hated.

I am afraid of a certain environment that sometimes arises when
it seems everyone is on the edge of a great cliff, or like animals
about to attack, looking for someone or something to gnash
their teeth into, to raise their claws at.

I am afraid of forgetting. Since I was born I have been forgetting. Forgetting what I have wanted to remember.

Sometimes it is necessary to have a quiet space in which to work fear out. One can be alone for many hours in this space, pulling fear from each limb, beckoning it out of the body, until it has been pulled all the way through.

Then, washing each limb in a basin, turn it over: shinbone, be mine again, do not belong to fear. Breastbone, cleansed.

I am much less afraid than I was before. Even death now does not seem so terrifying.

I have worked at this, arranged and rearranged my feelings on the subject, taken each feeling out and looked at it, turned it over in my palm.

Though the deepest fear it seems comes from the

GLARE

In an interview, Anne Carson says:

I do think that something of the effect I have on people is to put everything on an edge where they're both infatuated with a kind of charmingness happening in the person or in the writing, and also flatly terrified by a revelation or acceptance of revelation that's almost happening, never quite totally happening.

The interviewer calls this a kind of glare.

I imagine Anne Carson looking directly at me with this glare—glare of intensity and insistence that calls into awareness all the eeriness of being, its unacceptable finiteness.

When the interviewer asks her what that glare is, she replies:

I don't know. It's just absolute dread. It's bumping up against the fact that you die alone. You think about that from time to time all through life, and it continues to make no sense against all the little efforts you make in your life to be happy and have friends and pass the time.

The glare, the glare, the stunning-stark awful stare.

Something death said once. Before you were born. Something you forgot. Something you now remember.

But even with the glare (it never looks away from you—though you may look away from it briefly, and you didn't know it at all as a child), it is still possible to

GLEAM

How much gleaming is possible?

I don't know, see how much you can do while you are here . . .

    Say:

> *will gleam and understand,*
>
> *will gleam and understand,*
>
> *will gleam and understand,*
>> *[stir.*

I can see it streaming from you now . . .

It is coming off your teeth and heading toward the rest of the world . . .

It wants to gather with the rest of the light.

[be blown back]

be blown back   swells of stars   angels

            swarm

                        the skies   no one wilder   Sundays they droop

around   pretend to be human   silver

        dwelling   too close to God's huge and troubled

breath—

            hallowed room of his hand   love twines it

self   around them   held steady   invited

                out of love and pity

                                        the angels sing

                                down to us

I'm taking off my clothes now—

                        I've already taken off my shoes—

                                                        hands reaching

blown past

                the gliding rooms of youth

                                        where everything

                                                was wild and waiting

slivered light

spirit's slippery breathing

at the threshold

life / death

last earth-sweeping

I've heard the gong of life—

It struck me—

NOTES

"October Snow": The lines in italics in this poem are from Rainer Maria Rilke's "The First Elegy" from *The Duino Elegies*.

"Mary": The line of poetry mentioned at the beginning is from Karin Gottshall's "Travel."

"Self-Portrait through Glass": "How many people came and stayed a certain time . . ." is from John Ashbery's "Self-Portrait in a Convex Mirror." "Her leaving a doorway, light leaving a doorway" is from Anne Carson's "X. Vous Autre," in *Men in the Off Hours*. "Judge tenderly of me" is from Emily Dickinson's "This is my letter to the world . . ." "People who live in glass houses should not write poems" is from Vladimir Nabokov's *Pale Fire*. Muriel Rukeyser writes "be birds flying / be the enormous movements of the snows / be rain, be love" and many other beautiful things in "Night-Music." "Images classical and grand" echoes Sylvia Plath's "Child," which says, "images / Should be grand and classical." "My business is to sing" is also Dickinson's. "Dark and smart" is from Rainer Maria Rilke's "I Am Much Too Alone in This World, Yet Not Alone . . ." "Let everything happen to you: beauty and terror" is also Rilke, from "Go to the Limits of Your Longing . . ." "Will gleam and understand [stir" is a phrase that Dickinson wrote on an envelope. The interview with Anne Carson was published in the *Paris Review*.

ACKNOWLEDGMENTS

Thank you to the following publications in which these poems first appeared, sometimes in slightly different versions:

Amethyst Review: "[be blown back]"

Carl Sandburg Home National Historic Site website: "Dark Corner"

Center for Book Arts broadside: "church"

Conduit: "song," "[you were in the world]"

Connecticut River Review: "In Medias Res"

Intima: "All the Girls Were There, and Gorgeous"

Mid-American Review: "Do Not Hold the Birds," "October Snow"

Permafrost: "Mary"

Strange Horizons: "Lady Agnes"

Tupelo Quarterly: "On Beholding the Beloved's Rotting Body"

Some of the poems in this book were originally written as part of Tupelo Press's 30/30 Project. "On Beholding the Beloved's Body" was displayed as part of Montpelier's PoemCity. It was also a semifinalist for the Tupelo Quarterly Poetry Prize. "In Medias Res" was nominated for a Pushcart Prize. "song" received an honorable mention in the 2014 North Carolina State Poetry Contest. "Curtains" was a finalist for the 2015 North Carolina State Poetry Contest. "All Souls" was a finalist for the 2014 North Carolina State Short Fiction Contest.

IN GRATITUDE

I am thankful to the Vermont Arts Council, the National Endowment for the Arts, and the Vermont Community Foundation, for a Creation Grant to work on my manuscript, a gift that acted as an affirmation.

I am grateful for support from the Center for Book Arts Fine Press Publishing Seminar for Emerging Writers and the Frost Place Poetry Seminar.

I am grateful to the Vermont Studio Center, a place of magic and synchronicity, which awarded me my first residency and the Henry David Thoreau fellowship to attend.

I am grateful to the Carl Sandburg Home National Historic Site for selecting me as their 2018 writer-in-residence.

I am grateful to the MFA program at North Carolina State University, my peers and professors, for allowing me space and time to work on my writing and the resources to develop my craft: many of these poems were written there.

To the teachers, mentors, friends, guides, supporters, inspirers, partners, kindred spirits, and family members who over the years I have received love and support from: what I receive from you makes my life whole and meaningful. Thank you.

To the following people in particular I feel an immense amount of gratitude and indebtedness: Chelsea Krieg, Jody Rambo, Jody Gladding, and Vievee Francis—thank you for your friendship, mentorship, and encouragement.

I am grateful as well to Diana Fenves, Allison DeVille, Meghan Finn, and Andrea Martin—for your warmth, literary comradery, and belief in me and my words.

I am grateful to my Vermont writing group, especially Kate Gibbel, and to the WINC program, and my artist group.

I am thankful to my parents Eric and Laura Kucharczyk, for allowing me, from a young age, to pursue my own interests. I would swing and sing and think outside for hours. This is the place these poems come from.

I am grateful to the University of Massachusetts Press for bringing my book into the world so beautifully, and to Mary Dougherty for guiding me. I am grateful to Juniper Prize judge Abigail Chabitnoy for selecting it and for seeing me.

I am thankful to you for reading it.

JUNIPER
JUNIPER PRIZE FOR POETRY

This volume is the fifty-sixth recipient of the
Juniper Prize for Poetry, established in 1975 by
University of Massachusetts Press in collaboration with
the UMass Amherst MFA program for Poets and Writers.
The prize is named in honor of the poet Robert Francis
(1901–1987), who for many years lived in Fort Juniper,
a tiny home of his own construction, in Amherst.